ABANDONED NEVADA

ALL THAT GLITTERED

SUSAN TATTERSON

For my "Huckleberry"—Nevada was quite the adventure!

America Through Time is an imprint of Fonthill Media LLC
www.through-time.com
office@through-time.com

Published by Arcadia Publishing by arrangement with Fonthill Media LLC
For all general information, please contact Arcadia Publishing:
Telephone: 843-853-2070
Fax: 843-853-0044
E-mail: sales@arcadiapublishing.com
For customer service and orders:
Toll-Free 1-888-313-2665

www.arcadiapublishing.com

First published 2020

ISBN 978-1-63499-231-2

Typeset in Trade Gothic 10pt on 15pt
Printed and bound in England

CONTENTS

PREFACE

Nevada's seemingly endless desert is both secretive and wide open—a paradox of sorts, and one that inspires infinite curiosity. Far from the flashing neon and twenty-four-hour gambling tables of the Las Vegas strip, much of Nevada's desert no-man's land is owned by the federal government.

With often more than 100 miles between towns, this isolated desert offers the ideal location for military test operations. So ideal, in fact, that since the Groom Lake facility (aka Area 51) was first established in 1955, it has grown from an area measuring just 6 miles by 10 miles to a staggering 4,500 square miles.

Many long-forgotten ghost towns surround this restricted area, and alien conspiracy theorists, rather than ghost hunters, have made it famous. Interestingly, in 1996, State Route 375 was officially dedicated as the "Extraterrestrial Highway" in conjunction with the release of the Will Smith classic *Independence Day*.

Exploring southern and central Nevada's ghost towns is a fascinating step back in time but would not be complete without a visit to the more modern Area 51 tributes. The Alien Research Center welcomes curious visitors with a giant silver alien, and the huge tin shed offers kitschy souvenirs and a vast array of alien books. A little over 30 miles north on the E.T. Highway, the unique Little A'Le'Inn offers thirsty travelers a refreshment break and a tow-truck with, of course, a spacecraft in tow—some things you really do have to see to believe. As the Extraterrestrial Highway is the only route from the ghost town of Delamar to Tonopah, these stops are a welcome and amusing respite from the miles and miles of desolate and unbroken desert highway.

I have traveled extensively throughout Arizona and New Mexico in search of the abandoned and forgotten, for this series of books, and Nevada shares much with these states; but one difference that stood out is the sheer distance between anything resembling an actual town—with gas. My usual concerns, when off adventuring, involve rattlesnakes, open mine shafts (because I am always too preoccupied with a possible photographic opportunity to watch where I am walking), and two flat tires; these were the least of my worries in Nevada. I have a new-found respect for how far my Subaru can travel on empty—75 miles and counting!

As with other states I have explored and photographed, Nevada's abandonments share much with their counterparts—without human intervention, they take on a life of their own and now possess a mythical quality. They tell their stories with light, color, and decay. They inspire us to imagine what went on within their walls and on their streets, and they have led me on a wondrous and thought-provoking journey into America's past.

Usually, my list of people to thank is very long; I run into and chat with so many people during my travels—but Nevada's ghost towns really are ghost towns. Their silence is meditative and their emptiness poignant. I met very few souls along the way, but those I did were, as always, incredibly helpful and generous with their time.

Walt Kremin, a very big thank you for opening your wonderful Gold Point saloon for me when it was clearly the end of your long day. Your graciousness was appreciated and I will be back to explore more of your fascinating town. To "Captain Kirk," a Goldfield resident: you are a true character with many tall tales to tell. I learned so much from you in such a short time—thank you!

My travels would not be the same, and my writing would possess many more wayward commas, without my awesome sidekick, Heather Moulton. We have driven thousands of miles together across the Southwest, and I expect we will travel many thousands more because of my abandoned location obsession.

For the first time, I have space to thank my awesome publishers—everyone at Fonthill Media! Their Abandoned Union series of books fit wonderfully with my decade-long photographic passion and I am very honored to be a part of it. I am also very grateful for their openness to new titles and I am excited and looking forward to Heather's and my new *Graveyards of the Wild West* series.

I am also looking forward to many more Nevada adventures. With over 600 ghost towns scattered across the state, I know I will be back. Until then, I hope these photographs inspire your curiosity as much as the places have mine. Keep adventuring!

~ Sue Tatterson
Gold Canyon, 2019

RHYOLITE

Towering three-story, carcass-like stone facades overshadow Rhyolite's silent main street, beckoning ghost town hunters and Hollywood location scouts. As a haunting breeze stirs the desert dust, it is difficult to imagine this desolate stretch of road was once the center of a bustling town with, during its most prosperous years, an estimated 6,000 residents. How a town, once touted as the "Chicago of the West," could boom and bust in less than a decade foretells the illusory nature of impermanence in gold-mining towns; while most were short-lived, few soared as quickly from the desert floor as Rhyolite, and none that have vanished back into the Nevada desert ever stood as grand.

In August 1904, Frank "Shorty" Harris and his partner Ed Cross discovered gold at what is now known as Bullfrog Mountain, just south of where the bustling town of Rhyolite would soon spring to life. News of the discovery spread rapidly and, in less than a year, the town grew to host a population of 2,500. Rhyolite residents enjoyed fifty saloons, thirty-five gambling tables, nineteen lodging houses, sixteen restaurants, numerous barbers, a public bath house, and a weekly newspaper, *The Rhyolite Herald*.

The initial, rapid growth continued when industrialist Charles M. Schwab purchased the Montgomery Shoshone mine in 1906. By 1907, Rhyolite had electric lights, water mains, telephones, newspapers, a hospital, a school, an opera house, and a stock exchange—all due to Schwab's investment and seemingly unlimited funding. Schwab was head of the famed Bethlehem Steel on the East Coast where he was notorious for his risk-taking ventures and opulent lifestyle. It was through his negotiating skills that Rhyolite was added to the Las Vegas Tonopah Railroad. Three railroads would eventually serve Rhyolite and the dilapidated depot still stands today, after a stint as a "haunted casino."

Rhyolite's Cook Bank building at sunset.

Rhyolite's demise was swift, but its dance with death was drawn out over several years. In February 1908, a British mining engineer returned an unfavorable report, concluding the mine was overvalued and there was little remaining of the high-grade ore that had once brought investors clambering to invest. Following the report, the mine that produced more than $1 million in bullion in the first three years of operation saw its shares plummet from $23 a share to less than $3. The initial nail in Rhyolite's coffin had been hammered.

As the mine's output slowed, businesses closed, including all three banks, and by 1910, there were reportedly just over 600 residents. The next few years at Rhyolite saw a procession of "lasts": in 1912, the last newspaper printed its final page; the last train left Rhyolite's station in July 1914; and the death knell sounded in 1916 when the electricity was shut off and the Nevada California Power Company removed its lines.

But where do ghost towns go? It is a question that often puzzles me as I am wandering among what few ruins remain, especially in once large and established towns such as Rhyolite. I gaze around at the vast surrounding desert, longing for even a hint of what was and settling for only echoes. I have discovered, interestingly, most of Rhyolite was quickly dismantled and moved to other towns in the throes of establishing themselves and not gasping for their final breaths. In fact, the original Miners' Union Hall now stands in Beatty, a town only several miles away. Beatty actually claims to be the town "where Rhyolite came to live."

Rhyolite may well have settled in Beatty, but the remains of its hey-days will live forever in Hollywood films—it is easy to see why. In 1925, Paramount Pictures

restored the Tom Kelly Bottle House, a house comprised of 50,000 bottles collected by Kelley in less than six months. Kelly used bottles obtained from Rhyolite's fifty saloons, and after completing the home, he raffled it off at $5 per ticket, making a handsome sum. The Bennet family, who won the raffle, lived in the home until 1914. Paramount, while filming *The Air Mail*, restored the roof and the bottle house became a museum of sorts, which is still operational today.

Not surprisingly, many B-grade horror films and westerns used the town as a back drop. More recently, the 2005 Michael Bay film *The Island*, a futuristic sci-fi, featured Rhyolite's main street and the towering remains of the three-story Cook Bank building. Ewan McGregor and Scarlett Johansson make a memorable escape from an underground colony, stumbling through Rhyolite's ruins believing them to be all that remains of civilization after a nuclear war.

A century of abandonment under the blazing desert sun and the oftentimes blistering winds have created a desolate scene more realistic than could be imagined or replicated in a Hollywood studio. What another 100 years of neglect and exposure to such unforgiving elements will leave of Rhyolite is anybody's guess. The likelihood of anything remaining, other than piles of rubble, is slim. Rhyolite, as it stands today, has been immortalized in Hollywood feature films. The elegant ruins tell the tale of a town destined for demise—built upon the fabrication of glorious riches, like so much of Nevada—Rhyolite's collapse was as guaranteed as the sun scorching the desert landscape.

The Porter Brother's store ruins.

A new moon rises over the rubble.

Rhyolite Train Station Depot. It operated as a "haunted casino" for several years after Rhyolite was deserted.

The south-facing entrance to Rhyolite station.

The exterior of the jail.

The noon sun casts a shadow across the old jail.

The heavy steel door to the jail.

A collapsed residence looking toward the ruins that line Rhyolite's Main Street.

Above: An old wooden Union Pacific rail car.

Opposite page: The interior of the rail car.

Looking out from a mining tunnel entrance.

A mine tunnel leading back into the hillside.

Above: All that remains of one of Rhyolite's schools.

Opposite page: Crumbling stairs at the entrance to the former Cook Bank.

The Cook Bank ruins reflected in the window of a semi-restored building.

The exterior of the Tom Kelly Bottle House, which is now a museum.

The interior of a former residence.

Entrance to a mining tunnel.

The Nevada desert is littered with hundreds of dangerous former mines, of which Rhyolite has many.

An aerial view of Rhyolite's ruins looking toward the train depot.

The Cook Bank building was once three stories high with a basement. In 1908, it cost $90,000 to build.

The elegant facade of the Cook Bank stands resolutely on Rhyolite's main street. Its imposing structure has featured in several Hollywood films.

Rebar juts out of the crumbling ruins.

Looking west toward Death Valley from the old school building.

GOLD POINT

Ghost towns need saviors. These iconic remnants of our past are mysterious time capsules etched indelibly into the American psyche. Their fates typically take one of two paths: they collapse silently back into the Southwestern desert, or a soul in search of a lifestyle so remote and disconnected it settles in to salvage what a much hardier generation of explorers left behind. The story of Gold Point is as much the story of Walt Kremin as it is the town he has called home for almost half a century.

Due to the discovery of lime deposits in 1868, Gold Point was first established as Lime Point. Silver ore was uncovered in the early 1880s, but the remoteness of the location made it impractical for mining to continue, and by 1882, the camp was all but abandoned. It was not until early 1908 when high-grade horn silver was found that the mining camp became a town. The Hornsilver post office was established and the *Hornsilver Herald* began publication. The *Herald* proclaimed the former Lime Point, now Hornsilver, would soon become "the brightest star in Nevada's crown." Hornsilver quickly flourished and, at one point, its streets were home to over 225 wood-frame buildings, including, of course, thirteen saloons. As swiftly as the town had been reborn, it was soon deserted again. Litigation due to claim jumping and the ore body not living up to expectations saw most residents move on by 1909.

Mining operations began again in 1915 but failed to garner any traction, and the town's primary mine, The Great Western, went into receivership. In 1922, the mine was purchased at a receiver's auction by New York Giant's owner Charles Stoneham. Gold was discovered in 1927 and soon the town had not only a new lease on life, but another change of name—to Gold Point.

World War II saw the cessation of all mining activities at Gold Point, and after the war, although mining resumed, it was on a much smaller scale. Gold Point continued as a gold mining town into the 1960s, but the collapse of one the mine's main shafts caused the mine to close permanently and the town to became all but a ghost town. Gold Point's story should end here, as it has for so many former mining towns, but it does not; in fact, it continues to the present day.

In 1973, as fate would have it, Gold Point and Walt Kremin's destinies collided. The isolated little ghost town cast a spell on Walt, and he soon er listed his brother, Chuck, and friend, Herb Robbins, to begin buying buildings around the town. They worked hard restoring the historic buildings and creating a wonderful sense of the past. Fortune smiled on the business partners when, in 1997, Robbins won over $200,000 on a slot machine in Las Vegas. The men decided to use the money to establish Gold Point as a bed-and-breakfast, and today, although Robbins is still a resident, Walt runs it alone.

The town attracts curious visitors from all over the country, and although Kremin is solitary by nature, he graciously welcomes weary travelers to his little town. The restored mining huts offer basic but comfortable accommodations and the saloon is a barfly's Disneyland. The sheer amount of historical paraphernalia contained within its walls is a sight to behold. The town's streets offer a bounty of mining artifacts and the ghosts of prospectors are rumored to still wander them after dark. Decades ago, Gold Point found, in Walt Kremin, the key to its survival and Kremin in turn found his escape from the modern world. Together, they have created a portal to Nevada's mining heydays.

The Gold Point Post Office.

The remains of a wagon train and more modern vehicles at sunset.

Intact fencing around an old tin building.

The interior of a disintegrating building.

A miner's former home with views across the Nevada desert.

An old table in danger of collapsing.

Antique items from another era.

An old Wedgewood stove.

A welcome sign to Blood River.

An old-style bike with no modern additions.

The Ohio Mill building.

The interior of the Ohio Mill building is surrounded by disused mining equipment.

The Ohio mine was originally called the Great Western Mine.

What was once a cross-street in Gold Point.

A dirt road winds through Gold Point then heads out into the never-ending desert.

A former Gold Point resident's home.

Peeling paint, a lonely chair, and a stack of books inside the home.

An artifact from the Ohio Mine.

Discarded mining relics line Gold Point's dusty streets.

Heavily rusted machinery glowing in the late-afternoon sun.

A failing home and what remains of a clothesline—surrounded by a barren landscape, they paint a lonely picture.

GOLDFIELD

Late to the gold rush era in Nevada, Goldfield grew swiftly and dramatically to become the jewel in the crown of Nevada's mining settlements. So enamored by the town's gold laden ore, J.W. Scott was inspired to write:

Splendid, Magnificent, Queen of the Camps,
Mistress of countless Aladdin's lamps
Deity worshipped by kings and tramps,
The lure she is of the West.

And lure she did! From the initial discovery of float gold in the fall of 1902, Goldfield, by 1907–8, had a population of over 20,000 and held the honor of being Nevada's largest town and richest mining district. In 1906-07, alone, the town's mines produced more than $15 million.

Just 30 miles south of Tonopah, the first-laid claims near Rabbit Springs were called Sandstorm and Grandpa; the former, due to the swirling dust storm that enveloped two young prospectors, Billy Marsh and Harry Stimler, and the latter in the hopes it would become the granddaddy of all camps—which it did, but under the much more alluring name of Goldfield.

After an inauspicious start, Goldfield underwent a full-blown mining frenzy. Beginning in 1904, the multitudes descended from far and wide using whatever travel means they could secure: wagons, horses, a few automobiles as well as simply their own feet. The *Goldfield News* began publication and proclaimed Goldfield as the greatest camp ever (many other town's newspapers of the era made the same proclamation). The explosive growth continued, and during 1905, stately adobe brick and stone buildings began lining the cross streets and carpenters were kept busy twenty-four hours a day constructing frame houses.

Unlike other short-lived Nevada mining towns scattered throughout the uninhabited desert, Goldfield thrived for almost two decades. Electricity and water connections spurned more permanent development, including the four-story $450,000 Goldfield Hotel. When the hotel was completed in 1908, three days and nights of dancing and popping of champagne bottles ensued. Even San Franciscans flocked to the area; they were transported without a change of train in Pullman sleeping carriages and met at the depot by taxis ready to whisk them to the hotel.

Goldfield's history is voluminous. With a population of more than 20,000, it was inevitable that the best and worst of human nature would become exposed.

Heated labor battles rocked the town and greedy high-graders pocketed millions using specially designed overalls, false-soled shoes, and hollow pick handles. A world lightweight title between Joe Gans and Oscar "Battling" Nelson was fought at Goldfield bringing the town even more publicity and thousands of visitors.

The thriving metropolis also drew two of the West's famous Earp brothers, Wyatt and Virgil. In January 1905, Virgil was sworn in as deputy sheriff for Esmeralda county but sadly by October of the same year he passed away, at Goldfield's St. Mary's hospital on October 19, of pneumonia.

It is hard to imagine a town with such an invested population and impressive list of amenities, including five banks, two daily and three weekly newspapers, two mining stock exchanges, three railroads, and four schools, could cease to exist and become, what can only be described as, a semi-ghost town. Today, in 2019, the population, according to a local, is less than 100, although during the winter months, it supposedly swells to almost 200 with the arrival of winter visitors.

What happened? Where did Goldfield go? It was not packed up and moved on from like so many other towns. Its ore production did dwindle to negligible amounts, but that turned out not to be the cause of its demise. Fate chose to deal Goldfield two devastating blows—the second and final one it would never recover from.

Devastation first arrived in 1913 when a cloudburst flooded much of the town and many homes were left beyond repair after the water tore away their very foundations. The mining continued, though, as did many of the businesses. However, a decade later, in 1923, a fire tore through Goldfield and decimated 53 square blocks of the city and became known as the "great fire." A year later, in 1924, another fire destroyed the Goldfield News Building and the Montezuma Club. The fires ended Goldfield's illustrious days; the town was never rebuilt and what remains today gives scant indication of what was.

Goldfield glittered longer than most, if not all, of its counterparts. Today, restoration efforts are led by passionate members of its historical society and residents with the grit and determination needed to bring icons as grand as the Goldfield Hotel back to life. Their struggles are real and a sign outside the hotel begs for carpenters and plumbers. Goldfield will continue, in one form or another, but never again will it be the *"Splendid, Magnificent, Queen of the Camps."*

Previous page: The Goldfield Hotel, in the process of renovation.

Opposite page: The Thomas G. Lockhart House is situated on the corner of Euclid and Elliott Streets.

EUCLID
ELLIOTT

A dilapadated Goldfield home.

Jennie B. Elder House.

The Brown Parker Garage.

A series of "cribs" housed in a building situated in Goldfield's tenderloin district.

Beets Garage, built in 1930 after the fires.

Goldfield's first jail is situated on First Ave. and Elliott St. and was used until 1908.

A kitchen table and chair in an abandoned home have seen better days.

A recliner gathers dust as the aftrenoon sun streams through the curtains.

A gathering of mismatched chairs and a couch surrounded by personal belongings.

A badly water-damaged bedroom.

Above: A still-life scene in an abandoned bathroom.

Opposite page: A sink, where it has been many years since water has run.

Decades of dust cover a 1986 calendar and an old broom.

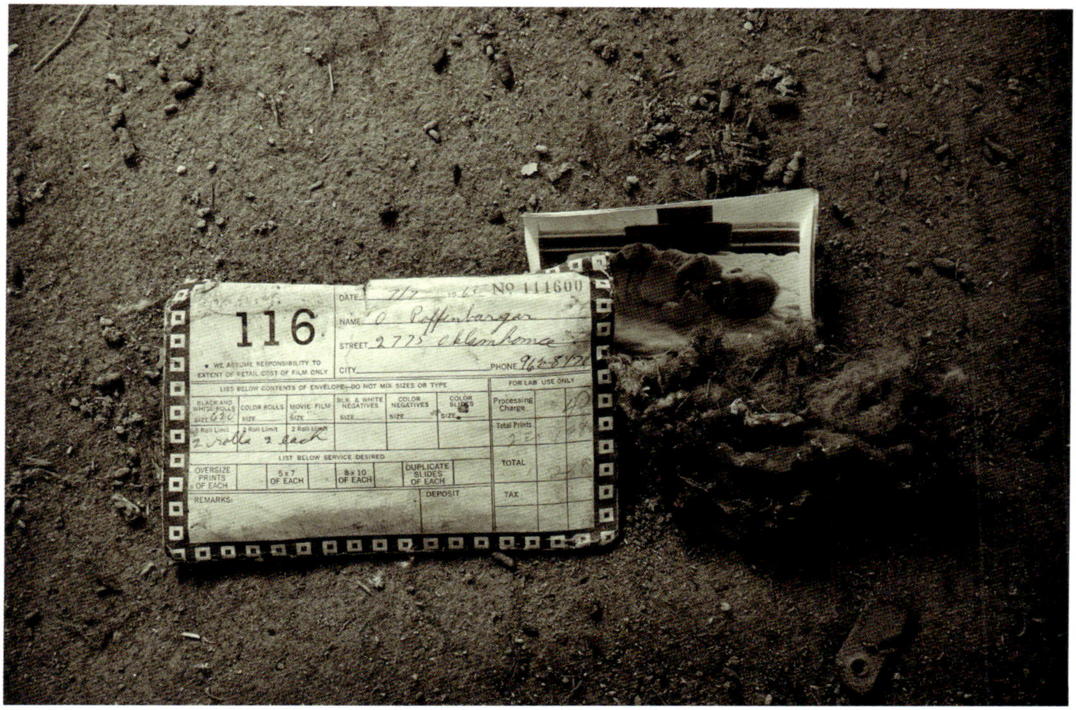

A photo packet from 1965 containing baby photos.

An old baseball cap on the back of a couch.

An old rusty Ford.

A row of vintage cars behind the main street.

A Pontiac Superior Ambulance.

The inside of the ambulance.

Above: A collapsing frame house.

Opposite page: Rotting furniture inside the frame house.

One of the few remaining structures in Blair.

BLAIR

The siren-song of the desert lures with not only the promised riches beneath its surface but also with a mirage-like glow dancing upon its surface. High on a peak, overlooking Clayton Valley, sits what was once the mining town of Blair and the ruins of its massive mill. To the west, far off in the distance, a shimmering blue plays games with the mind—and the eye. One hundred years after Blair was abandoned—the precious metals below the surface exhausted—a phenomenon, occurring in very few places across the globe, is proving to be extraordinarily productive and is clearly visible from the all but forgotten ghost town.

The Clayton Valley Lithium project has been in operation since 1966, but in 2018, further deposits of lithium bearing claystone were discovered. The net present value of the site is reportedly almost $1.5 billion; the $7 million produced at Blair by the Pittsburgh Silver Peak Gold Mining Company pales in comparison. A true anomaly, its briny waters shimmer as sparkling blue as the deepest of oceans in a dusty, brown, barren area of the Nevada desert.

Blair was established in 1906, when inflated land prices at nearby Silver Peak, drove the Pittsburgh Silver Peak Gold Mining Company to survey an area only three miles north. Within a year the company built the, then, largest mill in the state and a busy mining town soon sprang to life; saloons, a two-story hotel, a mercantile and a post office served the 700 residents. Today, only a dusty footprint of the mill and a few scattered buildings remain as a reminder of its existence.

By 1915, the ore had been exhausted and the town was deserted; the mill was dismantled and moved to California. The 17½-mile railroad, which once extended to the Tonopah and Goldfield main line, was torn up and the post office moved to Silver Peak, where it still operates today. By 1916, the town was completely abandoned.

If not for Nevada historical marker No. 174, on State Route 265, Blair's former location would rarely be accessed. The remains of the town exist where no official

The hill where Blair's mill once stood overlooking Clayton Valley with the mirage-like Lithium project visible in the distance.

road leads, and Google Maps struggled (and failed) to find the entrance. Blair was by no means a large town in comparison to neighboring Rhyolite and Goldfield, but it was still large enough for it to be difficult, in our modern era, to comprehend the impermanence of the early West.

The Clayton Valley Lithium Project.

A chimney stands proudly among the ruins of a stone building.

The ruins of the Blair Mill. The mill was once the largest in Nevada.

Desert plants are reclaiming the ghost town of Blair.

Above: Looking out toward Clayton Valley from the skeleton of a former Blair building.

Opposite page: Another view of Clayton Valley.

The slowly vanishing ruins of Blair.

The remains of a two-story Blair structure.

Ruins framed by other ruins.

A visitor's firepit beside the original fireplace.

A smaller building's wall shows signs of collapsing.

One of Blair's more extensive ruins.

A panoramic view of Blair's ruins with the mill site visible in the distance.

TONOPAH

Tonopah, a central oasis in the never-ending miles between lonely desert towns, beckons the weary traveler with oddly "famous" accommodations. The Clown Motel, named "America's Scariest Hotel" is home to more than 600 clowns, many of whom you will share a room with should you muster up the courage to spend the night. A little further down the road, the historic Mizpah Hotel is home to much paranormal activity and is the residence of a ghost known simply as the Lady in Red. There are two widely accepted theories to her identity. One claims she was a prostitute, who was beaten to death on the 5th floor by a jealous boyfriend, the other that she was a married woman caught cheating when her husband returned to the room after missing a train.

While Tonopah does not qualify as a true ghost town, only reminders of its bustling past remain. Many businesses along the main street are shuttered; the backstreets are dotted with abandoned homes; and the headframe of the Silver Top mine looms over the town, a disused relic of the town's illustrious mining past.

Many mining towns share a similar founding story—that of the happy accident. Tonopah's riches were discovered, so the story goes, by Jim Butler, an area rancher. In May 1900, Butler spent the night at Tonopah Springs, an area once used as a campground by Native American tribes. His mule had wandered off during the night and while Butler was searching for the roaming beast, he came upon an outcropping of silver-laden quartzite.

Initially Butler's find was discounted as worthless by a local assayer in nearby Klondike. Butler, though, had his doubts; he collected more samples on the return journey to his ranch and laid them out on a windowsill. The story then continues

The Clown Motel's bright welcome sign framed by the interior of an abandoned pick-up truck.

that not too long after, Tasker Oddie, the future governor of Nevada, stopped by. He spied the ore samples and offered to pay for another assay—Butler agreed and offered Oddie a quarter share interest in the assay.

Oddie's gamble paid off. The second assayer returned a finding that the ore in fact was worth $600 a ton. Butler was slow to act, but on August 27, 1900, he and his wife filed eight claims in the area surrounding the springs. Six of those claims would later turn into some of Nevada's most prosperous. From the period 1900 to 1921, almost $121 million in gold, silver, copper, and lead was extracted from Tonopah's mines.

Tonopah was settled as the town of Butler and grew quickly. By 1901, Butler became a stagecoach stop and a post office was soon established. The mines produced almost $750,000 in the first year, and the town expanded to serve its growing population by opening six saloons, restaurants, assay offices, and lodging houses. The town was renamed Tonopah in 1905.

For the next forty years, Tonopah operated as a bustling mining town. The Depression era slowed production, and by 1942, only four mining companies remained. A devastating fire in October of that year destroyed the Tonopah Extension Mill and by the end of the war all mining operations had ceased. In 1947, the Tonopah and Goldfield Railroad also ceased operating and the tearing up of its tracks tore what life remained out of Tonopah.

Today, the restored Mizpah Hotel is leading the charge to put Tonopah back on the map as the place to stay and break up the isolated seven-hour trip between Nevada's two major cities—Las Vegas and Reno. The town has its stalwarts who are working to ensure its future and The Tonopah Historic Mining Park Foundation is an anchor in these efforts. Both the guided and self-guided tours of the Mining Park offer a wonderful glimpse into the history of a town and its mines that were once the heartbeat of Nevada's settlement.

The Desert Queen Mine headframe.

An abandoned store on Tonopah's Main Street.

A once grand home turned meeting hall has been severely damaged by fire and is unlikely to be restored.

Tonopah's back streets are lined with abandoned homes.

The Desert Queen Mine hoist.

Inside the Desert Queen Mine hoist building.

The inner workings of the Desert Queen hoist.

Mining relics surround the Desert Queen hoist building.

Detail of a hoist wheel.

The Desert Queen's giant hoist wheels.

Vicenzo Lambertucci purchased a ranch, a mile or so outside Tonopah, in 1911.

A stone building on the Lambertucci property with a barn in the distance.

The smaller wooden buildings on the property were, reportedly, chicken coops.

One of the two barns on the Lambertucci property.

A view of the smaller barn from inside one of the stone buildings.

The interior of a barn on the 605 acre Lambertucci Ranch property.

Above: Mining and milling activities also took place on the property and can be seen in the distance from this failing wooden structure.

Opposite page: A collapsed tin shed with a barn in the background.

A clothes hanger is the only sign of life at a boarded up, abandoned Tonopah house.

One of Tonopah's many forgotten houses.

A shed in the rear of a house with a hoop-less basketball back-board.

Above: An abandoned Tonopah residence, where inside squatters had made a home.

Opposite page: Sunlight breaks through a covered window, highlighting the squatters bed and discarded straw hat.

Corn Show
County Corn Show

The former Tonopah Garage.

A Lincoln Continental parked permanently in the drive-through of the Tonopah Garage.

Discarded mining equipment.

A piece of Jaeger mining equipment.

Barbara Graham House, with a rail car in the background.

A desk and chair inside what was once the original warehouse for the Tonopah Mining Company.

Mining artifacts inside the former framing house.

An old leather shoe.

A well-worn glove.

The ruins that remain in Delamar are constructed from native stone.

DELAMAR

The dubious title of "The Widow-maker" was bestowed upon the remote town of Delamar—and not for the all-too-common gun fights of the era —but for the number of miners and millworkers who died from the lung disease silicosis. The dry mining technique, used to extract the gold from the quartzite, and the lack of available water caused the air inside the mine shafts and mill to be filled with a deadly fine dust. At one time, during the town's brief lifespan, there were reportedly four hundred widows.

Pahranagat Valley farmers discovered gold in 1889–90 and the mining district of Ferguson soon established itself in a treacherous and unforgiving area of Nevada's backcountry. Ferguson was so remote, building materials arrived, by mule train, from the nearest town 150 miles away in Utah. Tent towns made up most of Ferguson until in 1893, Captain John De Lamar purchased the principle claims for $150,000. De Lamar soon set to work developing the mines and founding Delamar.

By 1895, a 50-ton mill was operating, and numerous businesses were flourishing. The newspaper *The Delamar Lode* commenced publication in 1894 and a post office soon followed. For the next five years, Delamar was Nevada's premier ore producer and produced over half of the state's output. The boom years continued, although by the early part of the next century, Tonopah and Goldfield established themselves as worthy rivals in the ore production stakes. Delamar seceded its top spot as Nevada's premiere ore producer by the beginning of the twentieth century.

Providing an adequate supply of water to the town had always been a challenge and it proved to be a fatal flaw, in 1902, when a fire ripped through the town and destroyed all but the native stone buildings. There was not enough water pressure to fight the fire and much of Delamar was levelled.

The town was partially rebuilt, but two years later De Lemar sold his mining interests, after they produced more than $8.5 million in gold. Mining continued under the ownership of Simon Bamberger and in 1903, he installed a new 400-ton mill. Up until 1906, Delamar continued to outperform some of the more well-known mines, such as Bullfrog and Manhattan. The total production for Delamar was over $13.5 million

In 1909, major mining at Delamar came to a halt. Residents moved on to Tonopah or other nearby mining districts. Delamar's population peaked at around 3,000 souls, all lured by the promise of $3 per day in wages. Hundreds succumbed to silicosis, though the exact numbers are not known. It is a tragedy of the mining era to think they willingly sacrificed either their lives or many years of their lives for so little gain while the mine's owners reaped millions.

A crumbling stone building with the Hog Pen, the glory hole of the Delamar mine, in the background.

A view of the tailings dump from the ruins of a building.

A collapsed tin roof covers the stone rubble.

Above: The view across the valley from the mill area.

Opposite page: The ruins of a two-story stone building offers a view of what was once the tree-lined main street of Delamar.

Remains of the Delamar mill.

Large pieces of iron, which were once part of the mill, survive more successfully than the stone and wood.

A rusted out 44-gallon drum sits at the base of the mill remains.

The view from the Delamar mill site across the tailings dump and valley.

Wooden trestles at the top of a hill created by the quartzite dust.

NELSON

Less than 50 miles southeast of the glittering masquerade of neon that is the Las Vegas Strip lies another less showy fabrication—the ghost town of Nelson and the Techatticup Mine ruins. Today, the town known as Nelson is actually a little over a mile south of the original Nelson townsite and hosts several original buildings but most of them have been rebuilt and the cornucopia of historic artifacts and vintage cars have been brought in by the town's owners, Tony and Bobbie Werly.

Nelson's Techatticup Mine, established in the early 1860s was considered the oldest and richest of the Southern Nevada mines and notoriously as the most violent. Newspaper reports of the time credit the renaming of the town from Eldorado to Nelson to the murder of camp leader, Charles Nelson. Nelson allegedly fell victim to Ahvote, a member of the Southern Paiute tribe. Ahvote and another tribe member Queho are believed to have committed more than thirty murders over a twenty-five-year time frame from the late nineteenth through to the early twentieth century.

The number of killings attributed to Ahvote and Queho, while shocking, are also only claims, and it is difficult to discern the degree of truth in the numbers. A 1912 manuscript, *The Reign of Violence in Eldorado Canyon*, included in the *Nevada Historical Society's 1913 Biennial Report* and written by John L. Riggs, discusses Nelson's murder as well as many others not attributed to the Paiutes. Riggs, a resident of the area at the time of the killing of Nelson, and several others including Judge Morton, and the company's teamster Charles Monahan, charges that over a two-day killing spree, Ahvote did in fact murder a total of five men.

An old gas pump, a Texaco sign, and a pick-up welcome visitors to Nelson.

The number of murders, whether accurate or not, pale in comparison to the day-to-day mindless slaughter that went on between miners. The remote area attracted Civil War deserters from both sides and their disdain for the law and willingness to kill contributed to the legendary violence. In the 1870s, the nearest sheriff lived in Pioche, which was 200 miles north," owner Tony Werly explains. "It took him a week to get there, so not even a killing was a good enough reason for him to come."

Riggs, in his 1912 manuscript, describes the level of lawlessness in a town so remote there was no designated lawman nor any that wanted to venture into the area: "The mining law, at best, was a vague iridescent thing, about as open as a sieve; the real issues in equity were usually decided by 'Winchester's amendment to the Colt statute'; possession was always nine points of the law and usually all ten of them."

Twenty-first-century Nelson bears little resemblance to the rapaciously violent mining town of a century ago. While factitious tragedy is intimated by the remains of a plane crash jutting abruptly from the hillside, the crumpled aircraft is far from another chapter of death in Nelson's history. The plane is a Hollywood remnant from the poorly received film *3000 miles to Graceland*. Not surprisingly, the town's popularity with movie producers and photographers keeps the owners busy.

The Werlys purchased the land in 1994 and found themselves the owners of several mining claims, a store, a stamp mill, a bunkhouse, and a few tin miner

cabins, all in various stages of disrepair. As a carpenter, Werly worked tirelessly to restore the buildings.

The main building on the property, was once the miners' mess hall; now it is the head office and also used as a museum. It contains a plethora of historic pictures, mining equipment and other relics. As well as restoring the buildings, the Werlys have accumulated an enviable collection of artifacts, including many antique vehicles and memorabilia, all of which contribute to the town's popularity with photographers and filmmakers.

Ghosts are said to wander Nelson and the nearby Eldorado Canyon, and perhaps not just the ghosts of those killed senselessly during the heady mining days. On September 14, 1974, nine people were killed when a flash flood destroyed Nelson's Landing in the Eldorado Canyon less than a mile away from the Techatticup Mine. Torrential rain created an unstoppable wall of water, reportedly 40 feet high, that swept away everything in its path.

The power of Nature's wrath combined with the fury of those infected with gold rush fever left Nelson with a tragically auspicious death count. With the gold rush days long over and a flash flood warning sign now erected at Nelson's Landing, let us hope the demise of its remaining residents is due to natural causes.

Rain falls on a gas pump and one of the many abandoned vehicles.

A wooden spoked antique vehicle surrounded by rain-soaked cactus.

An old delivery truck.

The rusty brown of the fenders complements the post-storm sky and the desert mountains.

Abandoned pick-ups and other vintage vehicles surround Nelson.

An old garage with relics from another era, including a vintage Coca-Cola sign.

A tow truck outside a restored barn.

The tail section of the plane used in the film *3000 Miles to Graceland* juts out of the hillside.

Another view of the wrecked plane with the mountainous desert in the background.

A water tower frames an early twentieth-century vehicle.

A restored wagon train.

In stark contrast to the wagon train (opposite); an airstream and vintage car.

BIBLIOGRAPHY

"An Unmatched Boom." Travel Nevada, retrieved 2019 from travelnevada.com/discover/26440/rhyolite-ghost-town

Clayton Valley Lithium Claystone Project, Nevada, U.S.A, retrieved 2019 from www.cypressdevelopmentcorp.com/projects/nevada/glory-lithium-project-nevada/

Engh, Erik. "Blair, NV—Largest Mill in the State," Erik's Nevada Blog, July 2016, retrieved from erikjengh.wordpress.com/2016/07/08/blair-nv-the-blair-which-project/

Grundhauser, E., "A Short History of Area 51's Shady Expansion,"'Atlas Obscura, retrieved 2019 from www.atlasobscura.com/articles/a-short-history-of-area-51s-shady-expansion

"Historic Properties In Goldfield," Goldfield Historical Society, retrieved 2019 from www.goldfieldhistoricalsociety.com/historicproperties.html

"Nelson Ghost Town—Nevada," Kool Buildings, retrieved 2019 from www.youtube.com/watch?v=IkAgN7xeVjs

Paher, S. W. *Nevada Ghost Towns and Mining Camps* (Berkeley, New California: Howell North Books, 1970)

"The Legend Of Lady in Red Lives on At Tonopah's Mizpah Hotel" *Las Vegas Review-Journal,* retrieved 2019 from www.reviewjournal.com/local/local-nevada/the-legend-of-lady-in-red-lives-on-at-tonopahs-mizpah-hotel-1883112/

Third Biennial Report of the Nevada Historical Society, PDF. *Nevada Historical Society.* January 1913, retrieved 2019

"Tom Kelly's Bottle House," Atlas Obscura, retrieved 2019 from www.atlasobscura.com/places/tom-kellys-bottle-house

"Vacation In The Old West In A Real Live Ghost Town!—Located in Goldpoint," Nevada, retrieved 2019 from www.goldpointghosttown.com/

Weiser, K., "Delamar—The Widowmaker," Legends of America, April 2017, retrieved 2019 from www.legendsofamerica.com/nv-delamar/

Weiser, K., "Eldorado Canyon—Lawlessness on the Colorado River," Legends of America, March 2016, retrieved 2019 from www.legendsofamerica.com/nv-eldorado/